HOW TO SELL YOUR HOUSE FAST,

With Multiple Offers, For Thousands More Than You Hoped

CHARLIE MADISON

Jacobs & Whitehall
73-03 Bell Blvd, #10
Oakland Gardens, NY 11364
www.jacobsandwhitehall.com

Ordering Information:
Quantity sales. Special discounts are available on quantity purchases by corporations, associations, and others. For details, contact the publisher at the address above.
Orders by U.S. trade bookstores and wholesalers. Please contact Jacobs & Whitehall: Tel: (888) 991-2766 or visit www.jacobsandwhitehall.com.

Printed in the United States of America

Published in 2020

ISBN: 978-1-951149-58-1

Disclaimer

This publication is intended to be used for educational purposes only. No legal advice is being given, and no attorney-client relationship is intended to be created by reading this material. The author assumes no liability for any errors or omissions or for how this book or its contents are used or interpreted, or for any consequences resulting directly or indirectly from the use of this book. For legal or any other advice, please consult an experienced attorney or the appropriate expert, who is aware of the specific facts of your case and is knowledgeable in the law in your jurisdiction.

Benchmark Realty LLC
75 Industrial Dr, Mt. Juliet
TN 37122, United States
(615) 288-8292

TABLE OF CONTENTS

About The Author

I am a passionate and committed consultant focused on creating a memorable and profitable real estate experience for my clients. My entire business revolves around the idea of "leading with the giving hand" and offering help without any expectation of return. My goal is to carefully guide people through this journey, one person at a time, while keeping each and every person safe along the way. I believe that you need someone who represents your interests more than their commission check. I take every opportunity I can to be an investment in your life, not an expense. My entire focus is on providing so much value to your real estate experience that you'll cheerfully introduce me to the people you care about over and over again.

I will give you advice based on real experience, as well as the benefit of knowledge from regularly connecting and training with some of the brightest minds in the industry. You'll notice that I often answer the questions before you have them, because you, like me, don't want any surprises as you go through this very important journey.

Finally, I acknowledge that I periodically lose business because I don't always tell people what they want to hear; I tell them the truth, because they deserve it, and you deserve it. If this sounds like the kind of experience you're looking for, then I welcome you to be a part of our "Client Family".

CHAPTER 1

HOW TO SELL A HOUSE FAST FOR TOP DOLLAR

How can I almost guarantee two offers (or more) on your home, its first weekend on the market? By knowing how to leverage the right marketing strategy during the launch process—the same marketing strategy that leads to lines of people out the doors of Apple stores, all clamoring to get their hands on the newest iPhone. When I market a house, I want to do it in a way that makes people clamor to bid.

The secret to making this happen relies on a pretty simple rule: build up as much anticipation for the open house as possible, and then hold it only *once*, for a *limited period of time*. In my experience, this is the only way to hold an open house if the purpose of doing so is to actually sell the house.

So, what's the goal of holding multiple, large open house events like the ones often shown on TV? While many people think it's to help sell the house, only about four percent of homes are sold in this way; the truth is that it's to help the realtor find more clients. In fact, many new realtors will ask sellers if they can host open house events for the purposes of finding clients. Any realtor who's been in business for any length of time knows that holding an open house isn't likely to help them sell the house unless they do it at one specific time.

Simply drumming up anticipation of an open house and creating a sense of urgency can be enough to get at least one good offer on the table. For example, if a potential buyer is interested in seeing a house on Friday, and you let them know that an open house will be held on Sunday afternoon, they might be more likely to put in an offer right away, before the open house.

This works because the public believes that open houses sell homes. I've received countless offers in this way, and I've found that it doesn't hurt to oblige them and say, "Get your offer in as soon as possible, and I'll show it to the seller as soon as possible." Urgency makes a difference in sales.

CHAPTER 2

SELLING HOUSES: THE NUANCES EVERY REALTOR SHOULD KNOW

Time Limit Tactics

Most open houses last for two or three hours, but I limit mine to a strict 30-minute window, from 2pm to 2:30pm. Why? Other realtors have the same question, along with comments about how strange and unheard of it is. Funny enough, it's precisely that response—the one of surprise and curiosity—that I'm looking for. My goal is to generate attention on the house and make the open house event stand out from all the others; limiting it to 30 minutes is a great way to do this.

Perhaps even more important than the generation of attention is the dynamic it creates among potential buyers. With only 30 minutes to view the house, the chances of each potential buyer seeing every other potential buyer is high. This is useful because of one simple truth: people want what other people want.

Amid the rather frenzied environment created by a 30-minute showing, the ultimate goal is to get two people who want the house at the same time. When this is done well, I call it top-notch marketing. And it is this type of marketing that puts us in the control seat during negotiations, since all we have to say to the buyer is, "If you don't like the house, there's someone behind you who does. We're not going to budge."

Blind Bidding

When multiple buyers want a home, we can hold a blind bidding process, whereby each buyer is told that they have until a certain day and time to submit their highest offer. After that, the seller will be presented with every offer on the table and make a decision. Very often, this will generate at least one very high offer about an hour or two before the bidding deadline.

When the listing launch process is done right, it creates an environment in which buyers anticipate competition with other buyers, even if there are none. To avoid potentially losing the house, the only interested buyer will feel compelled to put in a high offer. It converts them from a tire kicker who just points out the flaws, to a buyer who's simply determined to get the house.

The Value of Home Staging

Some clients don't want to go through the whole launch process; they just want to be done with it, and they literally leave money on the table as a result. A good case in point is one of my favorite stories.

I had a client who had already moved out of a house that they wanted to sell. It needed about $15,000 of work put in, and with this in mind, we offered the house for $535,000 to an interested neighbor. After seeing the house in its entirety, the neighbor declined, saying the house was just too beat up for the price. We got the same response from an interested realtor who was initially very excited about the prospect of buying it. There was no way the neighbor or realtor would pay anything over $500,000 for it.

For $15,000, we replaced the carpet in a few rooms, painted it, had it deep cleaned, and took staging photos. We were ready to launch when that same realtor texted me and said, "Who did the staging? You're going to get over list price." He was absolutely right; we listed it at $580,000 and got seven offers in 48 hours, one of which was $600,000 with $18,000 in bonuses and no inspection.

Of course, all real estate issues must be disclosed, and this house wasn't free of them. For instance, we knew the pool needed a new liner which would cost about $5,000, as did the buyer. However, it didn't really matter, because there was also a backup offer from someone who said that without hesitation, they would have done without that $5,000 just to get the house. It was sold in as-is condition and it was a win-win situation.

Quality, Knowledge, and Pricing

A high-quality home looks good and has features that make it stand out from the rest. Most people are going to be in and out of a house in 15 or 20 minutes max, and they're probably going to be looking at five or six different homes. This means that even the smallest detail could make the difference between a great offer and no offer at all.

The goal of many buyers is to find flaws in a house; the goal of staging is to remove those flaws. Something as simple as painting certain walls a neutral color, rearranging the furniture, or pressure-washing the siding can completely change the look and feel of a home.

In addition to the quality of the home, it's essential to have knowledge of the local market. For example, there is a neighborhood in my area where half of the houses fall in one county, and the other half fall in another county. While this might not always make a difference, it does in this neighborhood because it dictates which school a child will go to. Since one county has highly-rated schools and the other doesn't, the price differential between the homes in each county is about $30,000.

A combination of quality and a solid knowledge of the local housing market it critical for knowing how to price a house well, and ultimately how to sell it.

Appraisals, and FHA or VA Loans

Every appraisal is a roll of the dice, because every appraiser works by their own set of guidelines. As such, no one can know for sure how those guidelines will be applied to a particular appraisal. With that said, it does seem that appraisers can be subconsciously influenced to make a higher appraisal on houses that they know have received multiple offers after the first weekend on the market.

Over the course of my career, I've become really good at selling houses over the appraised value, and I have never had a house appraised under the 30-day price. However, if we get a house under contract at the 60 or 90-day price, then I'll let the seller know that we may get it under the appraised value. If that ends up being the case, then these are the options:

#1 Drop the price to the new appraised value.

#2 Make the buyer bring cash to close for the difference if they can't get a loan above the appraised value.

#3 Meet in the middle of options #1 and #2.

By letting the seller know that this could happen and explaining the options, the element of unwelcome surprise is removed.

If a seller receives multiple offers, then they can go with a buyer who is going to pay cash, or whose lender's appraisal won't stick with the house for a long time. An FHA loan or a VA loan appraisal will stick with the house for three to six months. Knowing that every appraisal is a roll of the dice, I would rather have a conventional loan than an FHA or VA loan. Why? Because if the appraisal comes in low and there are multiple offers, then we can tell the buyer that they need to switch lenders and get a new appraisal, or just pay the difference. With a conventional loan, the appraisal is not recorded like it is with a VA or FHA loan, which means if they switch lenders, they can get a brand-new appraisal—potentially one that's higher.

Since an FHA or VA appraisal will stick with the house for three to six months, anyone who wants to buy the house with an FHA or VA loan during that period of time will use that appraisal. For some price ranges, an FHA or VA loan is virtually unavoidable, but the loan can make a big difference when there are multiple offers on the table.

While there is a process for contesting an appraisal, historically it's been difficult to do. Lately, however, I've had good luck contesting appraisals. I recently got an appraised value of $162,000 bumped up to $165,000, and a $209,000 bumped up to $210,000. In some cases, a low appraisal could warrant negotiations on the closing costs. For instance, we could agree to pay only a portion of the closing costs in order to account for the money lost on the low appraisal.

CHAPTER 3

WHAT MAKES A GOOD BUYER?

Source of Preapproval

Was the buyer preapproved by a bank that you're not even familiar with, or with a bank that has a solid reputation and that you've worked with before? This is an essential question to ask when considering what makes a "good buyer" and when choosing one to work with.

It is not uncommon for a deal to fall apart on the day of closing simply because the lender failed to check the necessary documents. This has been known to happen not only with low-level lenders, but large banks; some just have terrible bureaucratic processes. In addition, it's extremely helpful (albeit extremely rare) for a lender to have a direct relationship with their underwriter, because this means that the underwriter won't spring any surprises on the lender at the last moment.

No one can be forced to use a certain lender, but they can be incentivized to. For example, in exchange for using a certain lender and title, a buyer could enjoy a lower closing cost. This is an advanced tactic that only top strategic realtors employ, but it can be extremely useful when applied under the right circumstances with enough negotiating power to back it up.

A Choice of Buyers

If a buyer offers cash, take it; you won't have to worry about the appraisal at all. If there's no cash offer on the table, then next best option would be to choose a buyer who has a conventional loan. In our local contract, buyers state whether they have a conventional or FHA loan, and the size of the down payment. It is best to choose a buyer who offers a down payment of 20 percent or more, because this indicates that they have enough cash to cover the asking price should the appraisal come in low.

Three, Five, or 10 Percent Down

With a choice between a three, five, or 10 percent down payment, I would prefer 10 percent. The reason is pretty simple: if the appraisal is low and the potential buyer doesn't want to change appraisers, they will still have enough money to bring to the table. For instance, I recently worked with a buyer who I knew had 20 percent to put down, so they brought an additional $10,000 to the table and put 10 percent down instead of 20 percent. If, for example, they only had enough cash to put five percent down, then this would have been impossible.

Letters from the Heart

Some buyers choose to write a letter from the heart, which gives them a chance to personalize themselves and potentially stand out among other buyers. They might introduce themselves and the members of their family, explain exactly what makes the house so special to them, and include pictures so the seller can put faces to the words.

Letters from the heart don't always work, but sometimes they do. I once represented a seller who had five offers, and chose to leave about 1.5 percent of the purchase price on the table because he was so moved by a letter he received. He realized that he wanted the young couple to raise their child in the home—the same home in which he'd been raised. To him, knowing that this could happen was worth the money he left behind; it's not always about the dollars on the table. When a buyer understands this and feels moved to express themselves through a letter from the heart, they might just be doing exactly what they need to get the house.

Chapter 4

WHAT MAKES A GOOD LISTING AGENT?

Clearly-Defined Strategic Plan

A good listing agent should have a clearly defined, strategic marketing process and plan for each and every house they want to sell. They should know how to price a house well and high, and more importantly, how to sell it for that amount. They should also be prepared to communicate the details of their process to the seller, and avoid persuasion by the seller to list a house immediately when doing so would compromise the effectiveness of the launch process.

Access to Quick, Quality Repairmen

Staging can make or break a sale; a good listing agent understands this, and has connections to vendors who can ensure that it's done right. It's not enough to just know of good contractors, because good contractors are busy. Instead, a listing agent should have a solid rapport with several contractors so that the seller never has to delay the process of staging and selling their home. The listing agent should have a proven track record of helping clients identify what needs to be done, and then executing those tasks as quickly and efficiently as possible.

Knows Their Value (And Isn't Scared to Defend It)

If a listing agent is incapable of standing up for their own worth and making sure that they are paid what they deserve, why should anyone believe they would do that for their clients? It's fair to question a realtor's fee, and it's also fair to expect a confident response as to why that fee is well-deserved and can't be lowered.

While some agents altogether shy away from listing a ballpark figure for commission, I list the actual dollar figure that will go to me and to the buyer's agent. Why? Because I know that this is all people really care about: they just want to know how much money will be in their pocket at the end of the day.

On occasion, a client will ask me to lower my commission. To try to avoid this in the first place, I explain to clients up front that not all of the commission is going in my pocket; a portion is going to my broker, a portion is going to the buyer's agent, and about a third is going to Uncle Sam. As for the rest (and for the sake of a laugh), I tell them it just goes to my wife.

When there is still hesitancy on the part of the client, or if the client tries some light negotiating, I've found it helpful to just have a conversation with them and explain the value in what I do. "You don't want a listing agent who is going to roll over on what they do and who can't see the value in what they provide, because there's no way they're going to fight for your money if they're not even willing to fight for theirs," I'll say. And this is absolutely true, because the realtor is only going to get about three percent of every thousand dollars they make for the seller, but they'll get 100 percent of every dollar they make for proving their value.

Although I use the term commission here, when engaging with clients I use the term 'compensation' in order to drive home the point that I work hard for it, and that it is only by virtue of my negotiating skills, professionalism, and expertise that I earn it. I remind them that with me in charge, they're going to make more money, and do so a lot more peacefully than they would otherwise. A few of my clients have told me that what I accomplished for them was amazing, and that I'm underpaid for the work I do. Some clients have even given me tips on top of my normal commission.

Local Experience

As a listing agent, being able to read the underbelly of the local market, having access to the local multiple listing service (MLS), and using connections to other local agents can be extremely valuable. For example, a local agent would immediately know why the houses on one side of a neighborhood are selling for tens of thousands of dollars more than the houses on the other side of that same neighborhood, while an inexperienced agent with no knowledge of the local market would have no clue.

A Seller's Word of Advice (i.e. What a Listing Agent *Shouldn't* Do)

One of the leading complaints about agents is that they have poor communication skills, and as a result, leave sellers feeling unheard and uncared for. For example, many listing agents fail to provide sellers with any advice on which lenders to work with, or only make broad statements about "good" versus "bad" lenders. Is that useful information for a seller? I would argue that it's a lot more useful to have specific lenders in mind for specific types of clients and for specific reasons. This is the kind of informative communication that clients deserve, and by working closely with lenders and title companies, I can ensure that my clients receive it.

As another example, some agents will show impatience, and push for certain isolated actions (e.g.

posting a sign in the yard) without creating a real action plan. This not only leaves the seller without an idea of what to expect, but also indicates that the realtor hasn't taken the time to employ strategy in the selling of the house.

Seller Beware: "I will buy your house if I can't sell it"

Be wary of any listing agent who claims they'll either sell or buy your ***home,*** and ask yourself: are they making you sign a contract before they tell you how much they'll pay for your house? Will they show you all the costs up front? Have they even seen the house in order to know what the costs will be? Is it a contract you can get out of at any time with no penalty? In almost every instance of a listing agent or real estate company offering to either sell or buy a home, they are doing it because there's money in it for them—not for you.

Zillow and Opendoor are known for making offers which they claim are higher than a realtor could get. When I have a client that has received such an offer, I like to test out my marketing process; I tell them that if I can't sell their house for more than Zillow or Opendoor quotes them, then sell it to Zillow or Opendoor. Recently, my client was told they would make $2,000 less by going to a realtor, and what happened? My client made $18,000 more by working with me.

CHAPTER 5

SELF-SABOTAGING SELLERS

Self-sabotaging sellers make for really bad clients. So, how do people sabotage their own efforts to sell? In a number of ways.

#1 Thinking they know better than the realtor.

"My neighbor down the street sold their house for $450,000, so mine should too." Misguided statements of this sort are common, and fail to take into account the many factors involved in the value of a home. For instance, the year a house was built or the number of bedrooms it has can significantly impact its value, rendering a price comparison with any other house mute—even if that other house is right next door. When a seller believes they know the market better than their realtor, or that rumors about the selling price of nearby houses can inform them of the value of their own home, they set themselves up for a self-sabotaged selling process.

#2 Spending money on upgrades.

Good news: in a hot market, spending money on expensive upgrades confers no benefit. As a seller, all you really need to do is clean the house and make it look nice. You might want to do some yard work and plant some flowers, but don't replace the roof; no buyer will be comparing new and old roofs as a deciding factor (save this for the inspection).

If your house is really old and you want to sell it for top dollar, then you might want to repaint a wall or two, but don't put in brand-new luxury carpet in every room. You might want to replace a lighting fixture, but don't get a new HVAC just because the one you have is old; if it works, there's no reason to replace it.

Upgrades cost real money, but don't affect appraisals and will only leave you will less money in your pocket. And remember, when the listing launch is done right, there will be multiple offers, and when there are multiple offers, people become very willing to overlook old roofs and low-quality carpets.

#3 Not listening to the realtor's advice (yet refusing to lower the price).

As a realtor, it's my job to provide people with the expertise they need in order to sell their house for the highest price possible. It's in both our best interests to close a deal, because that's the only way either of us gets paid. In order to do my job, I have to be *allowed* to do it, which means I need a client who sees me as an expert and is willing to follow instruction.

In so many words, this is written into the exclusive listing agreement that every client is asked to sign. By signing the agreement, the client agrees to allow me to list and sell their house exclusively. This means that the client and I work together, and the client follows my advice regarding marketing, negotiating, etc. No other agent can be marketing the same house at the same time, because that just wouldn't make sense.

When I work for a client, I put 100 percent of my effort into attaining their goals, which means I am going to do whatever it takes to sell their house for the price they want. To accomplish this, I'm going utilize all of my best resources and vendors. If the client doesn't have the same dedication to our process, then it's not going to be successful and it wouldn't be fair to either of us.

I have a strategic system that works really well, but requires the seller's cooperation. It begins with a room-by-room review of their house and discussion of what needs to be done prior to the launch. A self-sabotaging and unreasonable client is one who says, "I'm not going to do these things, and I still want the top price."

For one reason or another, some clients will not want a sign posted in the yard, or any pictures of their house to be put online. When I'm presented with these types of sellers, I'm more or less being asked to do my job with one hand tied behind my back.

The prelaunch process through to the end of closing will require at least two and a half months of hard work, collaboration, communication, and mutual respect between me and the seller. There is simply no point in trying to make this process work when those elements aren't there. In short, if a seller is refusing to follow my advice and is maintaining unreasonable expectations, then I won't work with them or their referrals, because birds of a feather flock together.

Chapter 6

PICTURE PERFECT, ROOM-BY-ROOM

As the potential buyer approached the house for sale, they didn't like what they saw; they didn't like the driveway, the run-down mailbox, or the bland front yard. I watched them pull in, and then watched them pull right back out and drive away, without ever leaving their car.

While many sellers overlook the importance of these details, they are the first ones buyers notice. This is why every room-by-room action plans begins outside, where the buyer first lays eyes on the property. From there, we go through each room in the house, taking note of the things that would need to change in order for the house to sell fast, for the highest price.

In the past, I would complete room-by-room action plans by myself and just hand them over, but I've found that it's really valuable to complete them alongside the seller. This is especially true when the seller plans on living in the house during the listing launch process, because we'll need to discuss how to minimize the number of items in the house as much possible. This could mean selling furniture, buying a storage shed, or as a last resort, moving most of the items in the house to the garage. It's also important that there aren't any animals in the house, as this could quickly turn away some people (many clients will arrange to have their animals stay with a friend or family member during a showing).

On the listing launch weekend, I want the house to look like a model home; accomplishing this will mean selling the house faster, and not having to worry about keeping it in a "ready-to-show" state for more than a couple of days.

Not Too Much, Not Too Little

While the goal is to minimize the number of items in the house, it's certainly not to remove everything. I never want to sell a completely empty house, because completely empty houses reveal their flaws and blemishes. When there is a minimal amount of furniture in the main rooms of the house, people's eyes track to that furniture rather than to the smaller and potentially negative details of the house itself.

One staging tip is to put an air mattress with an attractive cover in one of the guest rooms. It's also a good idea to stage the master bedroom, kitchen, and living room with a minimal amount of furniture.

Photos that Pop

There's a lot of scrolling involved when it comes to searching the internet for homes for sale, and after a while, all the pictures start to look the same. There are also a lot of distractions in the world, which means it's even more difficult to grab the attention of someone who is multi-tasking during their search for a house that strikes their eye.

This is where high density resolution (HDR) technology can play an invaluable role in attracting potential buyers. It is an imaging technique that involves three photos in one: one that captures the darks of the room, one that captures the lights of the room, and one "regular" photo. The combination of these photos creates a very rich, surreal experience for the viewer—one in which the colors pop and everything appears flawless, like flipping through the pages of a magazine.

There are potentially hundreds of pictures for a buyer to find online, and not enough time in the day to give all of them a serious look. If the photos pop and catch their eye, and if the house is expertly staged, then there will be nothing stopping the buyer from showing up. Don't give buyers a reason *not* to give your house closer consideration; give them every reason to do exactly this.

HDR imaging can make the difference between a good offer in the first weekend and an empty open house. As just one example, there was a house that had some scratches on the kitchen walls, and the seller did not want to repaint. The concern was that potential buyers would be turned off by any photos of the scratches, so much so that they wouldn't even view the house. With the goal of at least getting potential buyers in the house, I was wise in my selection of photos, and only chose those which made the house pop with color and look impeccable. The result? In addition to having a lot of showings, we sold it for $20,000 more than homes of a similar size in the same neighborhood—and we did so during the second weekend.

Pictures are important; whether they inadvertently showcase a house's flaws or make it appear convincingly perfect, they'll have an impact on how many people show up and actually view it in person. This is critical, because not many people will buy a house without walking through it first (and those who do will want extra contingencies, which a seller might want to avoid).

CHAPTER 7

REAL TALK ABOUT REALTORS

You've been trying to sell your house for months, when you wake up one morning and find the 'For Sale' sign in your yard gone…not because you sold your house sold, but because your realtor decided to just pick up and leave with no explanation. Believe it or not, this happens. What kind of realtor does this, and why would they ever risk their reputation in this way?

The truth is that some realtors are actually trained to operate with this "Who cares if the house sells" mentality, because their only real goal is to use a seller's house as a means to finding more clients. In essence, your 'For Sale' sign is an advertisement for your realtor, not your house.

Other realtors run on a business model that's purely economical, and as such, the whole process of selling a home—from the strategic planning and prelaunch stages to closing—needs to be done as quickly as possible, even if that means short-changing you. These realtors are going to put a sign in your yard before putting any real work or planning into the process. They'll list the house as soon as possible, and encourage you to start with a low price. If they make you $10,000 and keep three percent commission for themselves, then they walk away with just $300. This poses a reverse principal-agent problem which requires the realtor to stay in business only by turning it.

There are also realtors who just don't have any clue what they're doing. They might be inexperienced and just eager to sell, or they might think the house will "sell itself." A house that's in the hands of a realtor like this could be listed for months without selling.

How I Do It Differently

Breaking a Rule

In sales, the overarching rule is to not walk away without a signature; I break this rule all the time, because I understand the importance of a strong, trust-based relationship between a seller and realtor. This relationship will last for three months, and it is in both people's interests for it to be one of peace and profitability. If the seller feels they were manipulated or pressured into hiring the realtor, or if they otherwise just don't feel comfortable with the realtor, then it will be a negative experience for all involved. I would much rather have a potential client take some time to figure out whether I'm the right fit for them, than to make a rash decision that ends up hurting us both in the end.

Communicating Proactively

For every house, I plan a custom launch process over the course of two to three weeks. During this process, I prioritize one of the most commonly-absent features of the relationship between seller and realtor: good communication.

To do this, I tell my clients that they can expect a call from me every week on Tuesday, regardless of whether there is an update. This not only creates structure for myself and the seller, but gives the seller peace of mind in knowing they can count on hearing from me regularly, which in turn reduces the number of nonurgent phone calls from clients on other days of the week. Of course, if they need to call me, I will answer, but proactive communication is key.

On Monday, I call all the vendors, the lender, the title company, and other agent to give my updates and ask for theirs. This is a great way to take responsibility for the transaction, and remain mindful of the fact that the other players involved are busy too. In some cases, I am able to coordinate communication between the other agent and title company or vice versa, which helps expedite and make the process more efficient.

This is something that benefits everyone involved, and might even result in an unexpected perk. For example, just last week, a client spoke to the lender and learned that they could move up the closing date by one week, which would save my client a lot of money. Had I not scheduled that Tuesday update call, I wouldn't have known this, or I would have found out about it too late.

The Monday and Tuesday calls establish and maintain communication, create accountability for me, ensure that everyone is in the loop, help me keep tabs on the timeline, and prevent misunderstandings that can lead to angry clients. A lot of realtors can't do this, either because they run on a churn-and-burn model or because they just don't have a clue what they're doing.

Timing the Close

When possible, I always close on a Tuesday, Wednesday, or Thursday during the second or third week of the month. The crux of this strategy is about gaining the full attention of the lenders and title companies, and thereby reducing errors and delays in the process.

Why do I try so hard to avoid closing on Fridays? It's because if there is a delay in closing, then the seller is out of the house all weekend, waiting for the issue to be resolved (this actually happens all the time). In contrast, if there is a delay in closing on a Thursday, it's not a big deal—it just gets pushed back by one day. There is a similar reason for not closing on Mondays; since so many closings are initially slated for Fridays, many of them get postponed until the following Monday, and we want to avoid the busiest times for lenders and title companies.

The motivation for closing during the second or third week of the month is the same: to avoid the times when so many other people are closing, and when all the lenders and title companies are extremely busy as a result. If a lender or title company is going to miss anything, it's going to be while they're busy, and if they miss a date near the end of the month, then it's going to roll over to the first of the following month. By closing in the second or third week of a month, we can get the full attention of our vendors, and set ourselves up for a much smoother, more efficient process. This is something that benefits everyone—the seller, the buyer, the lender, the title company, and me.

On closing day, the goal is to just sign the papers, and find no surprises. For this reason, I stay in touch with the agent, the title company, and the lender during the last part of the week before closing (i.e. the green zone). I want to make sure that everything is ready for the final walk-through and that there are no problems. If I do find problems, then I've already cleared my schedule to handle whatever is necessary.

Alleviating Seller Stress

Before I've even seen a house, some people will request that I email them "comps," which are comparable sales data based on the value of similar homes in the same area. The goal of this real estate tool is to help sellers determine how to best price their home.

If a client is considering selling and looking for a general idea of what to expect, then I'll view their house, create the comps, and walk them through a video presentation that will explain the price range and statistics. At this point, the range will probably be huge (e.g. $380,000 to $460,000) simply because we won't have narrowed down their goal in selling. Do they want to sell it super quickly, right now? Or do they want to take their time and put some money into it?

The point is, it's okay if the answer to these questions is still "I don't know," because the purpose of gathering the information for them is only to give them peace of mind in knowing that they have options, and roughly what to expect from those options. They might end up deciding to stay right where they are, but they might end up deciding to sell; if it happens to be the latter, then they already have a good framework for making it happen.

Digging for the Deeper Reasons Behind Selling or Buying

In my opinion, the client consultation is the primary and most impactful way to create the conditions for a peaceful and profitable transaction. For many people, this ends up being their favorite and most valued part of the process, and it usually comes as a surprise that it happens at all.

During these consultations, we build a list of all the reasons they want to move and all the features they want in their new house. If I'm working with a couple, then I'll ask each of them individually seven specific questions to drill down what they're really looking for. It might sound straightforward, but the underlying goal is a little more involved: I want them to access what they're really looking for, deep within their heart. This is a discovery process for people.

They might discover that they want land so that their kids can grow up in the same way they did, by having an amazing time playing outside with their siblings on the family farm. Or they might realize that since their kids have moved out, they want a simple place with landscaping provided so they can travel like they've always wanted.

Perhaps they want to spend their time visiting their grandchildren throughout the country, and taking those vacations they never could before, all without worrying about the house. These types of reasons are buried a bit deeper than just wanting the best deal, or just wanting the process to be painless, and it's these reasons that I'm looking to find.

Always Eyeing the Big Picture

By digging for the deeper reasons why a client wants to sell or buy a house, I can learn what is personally important to them, which helps me to forge an emotional connection with them. This works to my benefit when making tough recommendations that the seller might not otherwise want to follow. For example, I can say, "Hey, I know you don't want to paint this room, but I also know it's important for you to get as much money as possible so that you can finally do the traveling you have been dreaming about."

This can put things back in perspective for the seller, which is especially important during negotiations. It's really easy to get upset about some costs here and there, like $400 for new curtains or $1,000 for some new lighting, but this only leads people astray from the big picture and their overarching goal. The truth is that it often pays to take the high ground and remember what's really important. If new curtains and a new lighting fixture means losing $1,400 but ultimately making $30,000 over the bottom price and closing within the month, then the seller ends up on top.

According to the statistics, the median transaction count for an agent is four to six per year, but I believe every realtor is capable of closing three or four times that amount. The problem is that realtors lose about a quarter of their deals just from poor negotiations, which are driven by getting lost in the weeds, losing sight of the grand scheme of things, and letting emotions get out of hand. A good agent is an expert and a leader who's always eyeing the big picture, and who doesn't let deals fall apart.

I've watched agents lose their cool, and lose deals. Let me tell you, it's not a pretty sight. I don't lose deals, plain and simply. And ultimately, it's because I take the time to really understand my clients and their big-picture goals. Equipped with that understanding, I can keep my clients on track to attain those goals through wise negotiations.

CHAPTER 8

THE PINPOINT PRICE ANALYSIS

The pinpoint price analysis is a range of prices for which a house will sell. This analysis involves a tricky balance of pricing high without overpricing. When a house is overpriced, it will be rejected, and when a house is rejected, it will remain on the market until the price has been lowered to a fair and appropriate amount.

Why is this bad? Because at this point in the process—potentially months after the initial launch—you will have lost your negotiating power. Just like the iPhone would have never been successful if Apple charged $5,000 for it, a house on the market won't sell when it's clearly overpriced. An example of what happens when a house is overpriced can be illustrated with a story from my experience as a realtor.

I was representing a client whose house had a pinpoint price analysis of $385,000, $400,000, and $425,000, which meant that even with our flawless marketing process, the most we were going to get was $415,000 or $420,000 (even that was a stretch). However, the seller insisted that his house was worth $450,00 and refused to budge on that price. The house needed at least $1,500 worth of repairs, but with ownership blinders on, the seller didn't agree; he believed the house was just as it should be, and didn't even agree to do any staging.

As the client wished, we listed the house for $450,000 and what happened is exactly what I expected: every potential buyer said it was overpriced and moved on to the next. Finally, we dropped the price to $435,000, but the response was the same: every potential buyer said it was overpriced. The seller didn't know why the house hadn't already sold, and the truth of the matter is that the price still wasn't even in the ballpark of the value of the house.

At this point, the house had already been on the market for over a month, which means the glamor had long worn off, and buyers were becoming suspicious that something must really be wrong with it. Eventually, we dropped to the middle point of the price analysis, to $400,000, and finally received an offer at the base price of $385,000. Had the seller not overpriced the house from the beginning, he could have walked away with an offer $15,000 or $20,000 higher.

30, 60, and 90-Day Price Comparisons

In essence, the pinpoint analysis and 30-60-90-day price comparisons provide the seller with a range of what they'll be able to put in their pocket at the end of the day, given a certain selling price at each point. In a hot market, the 30-60-90-day price points are really like two-week, four-week, and eight-week price points.

A 30-day price is usually a percent or two underneath the market value. While nothing can be guaranteed in real estate, there's really no reason a house shouldn't sell for the 30-day price within one month, even if the improvements or necessary upgrades aren't done. If a house sells for below my 30-day price, then I'll sacrifice my commission, and although it's rare, it has happened before. In almost every case, there is an offer over the 30-day price.

A house is likely to sell at the 60-day price, especially in a good market with a good listing launch. Within the first week or two—and maybe even after the first weekend—a house is likely to sell for the 60-day price.

The 90-day price is there for the purposes of being transparent and honest. While some realtors might try to hide really high comparable prices, I think it's important to disclose that a comparable house sold for an extraordinary amount. However, it's also important to explain that there may have been unique circumstances which made that possible, and that it's highly unlikely to happen again. The seller has the option of trying to list a house at the 90-day price, but they should be forewarned that it probably won't sell at that price, which means the house will remain on the market until the price is dropped.

In my experience, if a seller lists their house for any amount over the 90-day price, they're likely going to end up selling it for the 30-day price. Case in point: the aforementioned story in this chapter.

Early on in the process, I tell clients that there will be a pinpoint price analysis including 30-60-90-day price comparisons, followed by a discussion regarding the actual dollar amount of the real estate commissions, closing costs, title expenses, and mortgage payoff amount. I want my clients to enter the process of selling their home with confidence, knowing exactly what amount they could end up with after fees and real estate compensation.

In reality, my pinpoint price analyses are such that sellers walk away with more in their pocket than they expected. In fact, I don't think a single client of mine has walked away with less. With that said, I always ask my clients whether they are okay with the net amount. If the answer is no, that's okay; we can consider other options, like selling at a later time when the market has improved. I've worked with clients before who've chosen to do this, and they ended up making about $10,000 more.

Ultimately, I don't want there to be any surprises for my clients, especially as a result of me not being entirely transparent with the estimated take-home amounts. Many realtors are shocked to learn just how straightforward I am with clients in this regard. Listing agents might point to the lender or title company or some other entity as the reason for the estimates, but I know that people know that realtors need to make money—even the ones who say that's not what it's about. For the seller, the payoff is in proving your worth as an agent and making sure they walk away from the transaction satisfied, or better yet, thrilled.

CHAPTER 9

INSPECTIONS AND REPAIRS

I won't lie...I get pissed off every time I receive a buyer's inspection report showing what they want to fix, and I am sure that I have pissed off countless sellers by sending the same type of inspection report. Of course, if I'm representing a seller and there are multiple offers on the table, then it won't matter all that much, because we'll have the ability to say, "Look, we've got a backup offer that's willing to take it as is." However, that's not always the case.

In preparation of this, I set the expectation of about $1,200 worth of repairs. When I receive the inspection report, I won't just have my assistant pass it along; I will get on the phone with my client and we'll review it in detail. It's true that a lot of sellers will initially get angry and question every item on the report, which is when I will remind them to not lose sight of the big-picture goal. If attaining that goal means spending a few hundred dollars more than expected, it's probably worth it.

I'll also do everything I can to knock off as many issues as possible. For example, for every issue the seller claims doesn't actually need to be repaired, I'll help track down the documentation or receipt for that item. In many cases, an inspection report will list a repair that is necessary under the current code, but wasn't necessary under the code that existed when the house was built. If I can confirm this after talking with my contractors, then those costs can be eliminated as well.

Lastly, I'll try to negotiate with my vendors. For example, if there are a handful of small jobs that can be rolled into one project for a lower price, then we'll take that option. In fact, since my vendors do such quality work for such low prices, I don't even recommend that buyers ask for specific items to be repaired, because I know that we can get multiple projects done for the price of one. Furthermore, I know that if we ask the seller to have the repairs done, they are going to get them done as cheaply as possible, since they just want to maximize their profit. Here, we once again encounter the principal-agent problem.

Imagine that you're about to close on a $400,000 house after taking all the necessary steps, including the inspection and negotiation of repairs. All you want to do is feel the relief of knowing the house is yours, and begin the exciting transition into your new space. On the day of closing, you do a final walk-through just to make sure everything looks good, and you discover that the sellers did not do the $200 repair they said they would. That's a breach of trust, and at that point, you might have to delay closing just out of principle. Even if it all gets worked out and the sellers agree to write a check, those hard feelings may linger around the fact that the seller didn't stay true to their word.

Instead of even allowing this sort of situation to arise, we will have our trusted vendors do the repairs prior to closing day, bring the seller a quote for the repairs, and receive a check for those repairs at closing. This will not only make closing day much more peaceful, but eliminate the chance of a delayed closing. In addition, taking this approach means that it is not the buyer's nor my responsibility to understand every detail of the inspector's report and confirm that the issues have been fixed.

A Seller's Inspection Means Sunk Costs

Home inspectors get paid to find problems, and every inspector will find different ones. Even on a brand-new house, it wouldn't be surprising if an inspector were to come up with a handful of issues. This means that even if a seller spends money on the repair recommendations made by one inspector, a second inspector could still come up with the same number of problems—just different ones. In this way, repair costs could mean sunk costs.

Another reason I wouldn't advise a seller to preemptively get a home inspection—especially in a hot market—is because oftentimes, buyers will be turned off by the inspection report, even if every single problem has been fixed. We want to maximize the number of people who see the house in person, and risking the loss of even one potential buyer isn't worth it. At the end of the day, getting an inspection and making the repairs really doesn't help with the listing launch strategy.

Chapter 10

WHEN SELLERS ARE BUYERS

A client who is looking to both sell and buy a house, and who's working within a very narrow time frame to make it happen poses a special kind of challenge that I love: one that requires really good teamwork and strategy. Other realtors will tell these types of clients that they'll make sure they find another house before selling their current one, but often this won't happen. Instead, they'll find themselves in an apartment or Airbnb for weeks or months.

No one wants to find themselves stranded with nowhere to go and a giant moving truck packed full, but it happens. I've heard horror stories of people who have had to be out of their home by noon on one day, and couldn't be in their new home until after closing on that same day. As a result, they quite literally had a packed truck at the title closing company, and could only hope to god that the closing would go smoothly. Under these circumstances, everyone is left standing on pins and needles, and it's just terribly stressful for all involved. In addition, thousands of dollars stand to be lost, not just on paying rent for the interim housing, but on any appreciation that occurs on the house.

The simplest strategy for avoiding this is to sell the home with a home-buying contingency, which means we get the house under contract to be sold to a buyer contingent upon moving into another house within 60 days. In other words, the sale agreement is contingent literally up until the day of closing on the new home. This works best when there is demand for the house created by multiple interested buyers. This gives the seller time to go home shopping, without feeling rushed and without the possibility of ending up with nowhere to go.

The Double Down Payment

If a client has even five percent equity in their home, they can manage a double down payment on a new home. This is one of my favorite moves, and most people haven't even heard of it. We do this by partnering with a bank that provides amazing home equity lines of credit for five or more percent equity. The five percent equity is used as a down payment on the new house, and we tell the lender we want to do a double down payment.

At that point, the buyer can move into their new house while their old house is on the market or in the process of closing. Once the house closes, the money made on the sale can be used a second down payment on the new house. This triggers a recalculation of the mortgage as if a 10 or 20 percent down payment had been made from the start, with no financing fees.

Many people want to put 20 percent down on a house in order to get a lower monthly mortgage payment, but they can't because a lot of their equity is locked up in their current house. By using this strategy, we can access that equity before selling the house. In essence, this allows someone to buy a new home before they've sold their current one, and to use the entire amount of equity in the home with no fees.

If we can put a contract on the new home and immediately list the current house, then they can close on the house they're selling before they even have a payment on the new house. Alternatively, they could move into the new house before selling the current one, and while they comfortably settle into the new house, we will do everything necessary to prepare the other one for the market.

The double down payment using a home equity line of credit is an excellent way to make a 20 percent down payment without incurring any financing fees. It's my favorite method for ensuring profitability and peace in what could otherwise be a very stressful real estate transaction.

Index

O

P

S

V

Z

Notes

Made in the USA
Monee, IL
05 November 2026

67385062R00043